When You're the News

What to Do When You're Being Interviewed

by Rick Taylor

STANDARD PUBLISHING
Cincinnati, Ohio   3185

Library of Congress Cataloging in Publication Data

Taylor, Rick (S. Richard)
  When you're the news.

  1. Mass media in religion. 2. Interviewing in journalism. I. Title.
BV652.95.T39 1987   254.4   86-23143
ISBN 0-87403-225-3

Copyright © 1987, The STANDARD PUBLISHING Company,
  Cincinnati, Ohio.
A division of STANDEX INTERNATIONAL Corporation.
Printed in U.S.A.

To my father

Acknowledgments

During my ten years in television news, I met many wonderful professional newspeople who added much to my life. Some of them were Christians. To them all, "Thank you."

During the writing of this work, many people have been instructional, supportive, and motivational. I wish to acknowledge a few. To Robert E. Korth, the editor of this work, a sincere acknowledgment that it is he who chartered the course for the finishing of this project and without whom this would still be only in manuscript form. To those who commented for this work, dear friends, I hope to repay your kindness. And finally, to Ella Smith, a dear Christian lady, thank you most for when the times were the hardest. I love you.

Foreword

A certain portion of Scripture from Matthew 10 kept coming to mind as I read Rick's manuscript—"... be wise as serpents but gentle as doves." Being wise but gentle was an attitude mandated by Jesus Christ, and it remains one that can advance His cause throughout the world.

Sometimes Christians are neither wise nor gentle, making unChristlike statements regarding those they consider to be the opposition. U.S. Senate Chaplain Richard Halverson has said that the most condemning hate mail the senators receive is sent by "God-fearing Christians." All too often Christians forget that Jesus came not to condemn the world but to save it, often associating with people having far different views and values from himself.

It is no secret that the media leans to the left. In 1981 Robert Lichter and Stanley Rothman interviewed 240 members of all levels of the most influential news media outlets in the country. The survey showed that while 80% of the general public feel religion is important in their lives, fewer than one in five of the news executives polled ever attended church or synagogue. In 1985 *Newsweek* found only 21% of those polled favored abortion on demand, while the Lichter-Rothman report showed that 90% of the news media queried favored it. A recent *Time* survey showed that 42% of the Americans polled considered themselves to be conservative, 42% considered themselves moderate, and only 14% claimed to be liberal. America's news media, by a clear majority (54%) claimed to be liberal, according to the Lichter-Rothman report. Of the 97 members of the news media questioned about whom they voted for in the 1972 election (which gave Republican Richard Nixon a landslide victory), 82 said they voted for the liberal Democrat George McGovern.

The thinking of many newsrooms does not conform to Christian thinking, or even, according to the survey, with public opinion in general. There is a distinct difference between a basically conservative America and a liberal news media. But that difference must not keep us from conversing with the media, and in many cases even accommodating them.

Rick's book gives practical, helpful suggestions that can bridge the gap between Christians and the media. Rick suggests throughout the book that Christians put the media first, attempting to accommodate them, treating them with respect and *agape* love. He shows that we can do this and still stand firm in our faith.

This book needed to be written years ago. If Christians will read it and take its advice, their image with the media will improve and will also become more biblically based.

Be alert. Be cooperative. Be wise but gentle. This book by my good friend and brother in Christ will help you in accomplishing that.

God bless you as you read it.

John A. Adams
News Director,
U.S.A. Radio Network

Contents

Foreword
Introduction

1. The Problem 13
2. The Medium 17
    Reporters Have Wide Differences in Training
    Picture Scenes Dominate the News Story
    A Natural Appearance in an Unnatural Setting
    Egos in the Newsroom
3. The Messengers—TV Reporters 27
    Specific Traits of Reporters
4. Types of Interviews. 34
    The Office Interview
    The Press Conference Interview
    The Event Interview
    The Pseudo-Event Interview
    The Stakeout Interview
    The Talk Show Interview
5. Interview Problems and Needs 51
    Openness During the Interview
    Makeup for the Interview
    Anticipating Reporters' Questions

6. Personal Tips 55
    Be Unique
    Be Brief
    Be Informed
    Be Honest
    Be Helpful
    Be Hospitable
    Be Insightful
    Be Optimistic and Hopeful
    Be Factual
    Be Expressive
    Be Controlled
7. Other Television Opportunities 69
    Editorials
    The Church's Use of Video
    Public Service Announcements
    Organization
8. Radio and Print Media 75
    Radio News
    Ways to Enhance Radio Use
    Print Media
    Ways to Enhance Print Use
    Which Medium to Use?
9. Bridging the Spiritual Gap 88
    The Messenger and the Message
    Final Thoughts

About the Author

Introduction

At least three facts about our society have necessitated this book.

In an increasing number of instances, state and church have found themselves at odds with each other. More and more confrontations between the government and the church are being presented on television programs. Media-experienced government officials have too often received greater attention from news reporters because of their familiarity with the medium of television. Equally, too often those representing the biblical view have not been effective because of their lack of familiarity with the medium. When the inexperienced church spokesperson feels uncomfortable and tense, his nervousness is perceived by the audience at home. This reduces his effectiveness as a messenger for Christ.

Second, the church is becoming more active in social matters to counter injustice and sin. For this reason, Christian leaders need to know how to make the most of communications media, which are so effectively used by non-Christians. Church leaders need to know ways they can use media (especially television) more effectively. The medium is not bad, but its current use is. Christians can change this.

Third, Christians can provide a balance to the slanted, biased presentation of news from secular networks. The more effective the church is in presenting the biblical perspective to the mass audience through a secular means of communication, the more millions are reached with the Word of God.

If you anticipate being interviewed by the news media (and it's more likely to happen than you think), you should view the suggestions offered in this book with the same attention that you gave the first sermon you ever preached or the first class you ever taught. Even if you're an experienced public speaker, you will still need help preparing for a media interview, especially for television. It is a different medium, with different constraints and different freedoms. The difference between public speaking and speaking on television is comparable to the differences between flying a single engine plane and flying a Lear jet. A successful Lear jet pilot can fly a smaller plane. Yet many skillful preachers and public speakers think they can "pilot" the airwaves of television news without any training or thought about how it might differ from that with which they are comfortable.

This book is an insider's analysis of what television news is all about. Its guidelines are presented as alternatives to the ways in which some attempt to use television and other media. This step-by-step approach will help church leaders get a fair treatment on the evening news and represent the Christian perspective on our world more accurately. I hope you will refer to this handbook when you are interviewed by the media and that you will find some suggestions that will help you make your interview more productive.

CHAPTER 1

The Problem

Television has been taken over by worldly people for worldly purposes. When it began, television was used for family entertainment. Much wholesome programming was presented. Television news was presented with honesty, fairness, and balance. There was no effort to entertain with television news; the goal was to inform.

As television programming began to change in its content, so did television news. With ratings concerns, TV shows began to entice us with sex, violence, and indulgence in pleasure. Moral concerns gave way to financial concerns. The more risque the program, the larger the audience, it was thought. We now see this philosophy at its zenith. The top programs on television include Dallas, Dynasty, Knots Landing and similar programs where abuse, excess and "works of the flesh" (as Paul describes them in Galatians 5:19-21) are paramount.

The philosophy that transformed television shows into appeals to the flesh has worked a similar transformation on television news. TV news organizations are subject to ratings concerns just as entertainment programs are. Winning the biggest audience is the concern of television news directors, anchors and reporters. Their jobs depend upon gaining and holding the largest number of viewers. Without question, this basic concern determines their success in the television news business and affects what they do and how they do it.

On the first anniversary of the assassination attempt of President Reagan, I was anchoring the evening news in Cincinnati. On our 11:00 news program we showed a slow motion clip of the incident. Dramatically, viewers saw the President shot and then pushed into the limousine and driven away. Guards in slow motion tackled the gunman and wrestled him to the ground. The thirty seconds of videotape was moving and full of emotion as we relived that horrifying experience. Part of what added to the drama was the silence of the tape—silence, except for the clear sound of a single bullet discharging from a gun and the resulting image of a secret service agent reeling from the impact of the bullet. Powerful television drama in the form of electronic news.

Yet it was *not* real, even though what we had shown was the actual footage.

I had been so impressed by the impact of that clip that I turned to my co-anchor and said, "That was powerful. Where did we get that piece of tape?"

Her response was, "You don't know what was done?"
"No!"

She explained to me that the 11:00 producer had taken the videotape provided to us by our network and had removed the sound. In place of the actual sound of commotion, shouts and scuffling, the producer had arranged for another sound track to be inserted.

That day in Cincinnati, a bull had gotten free from the stockyard and had wandered downtown. Police cornered the desperate animal and ultimately killed him with a single rifle shot. The sound of that discharge was the sound viewers heard when they saw the assassination attempt of the president one year later on our evening news.

Dishonest? Yes! I was shocked to hear that a producer I had previously respected had fabricated the news to make a dramatic impact upon viewers. That producer yielded to the increasing demands of news organizations to make the news "come alive with excitement." The basic problem with what was done is that it deceives the viewers. The methods used start a precedent of altering the facts and the way they are presented, to make real life seem more exciting and worthy of our attention.

This example is not an isolated case. The whole of television, including TV news, "participates in our turned-awayness from God. It often dehumanizes people; it presents the idols of society in dazzling imagery; its monologue says that ultimate worth is to be found in the things of the world."[1] Television has fallen prey to a philosophy that manipulates, distorts and confuses reality to make it what we want to see (or what TV executives think we want to see). In the final analysis, television's "visage is one of friendly, open, earnest communication, a 'communication' with appearance of the I-Thou relation which in reality almost always makes objects of us all."[2]

The problem Christians have in dealing with television is the same problem Christians have in dealing with anything else in a sinful world—the world at best misunderstands us and at worst hates us. Further, those of the world (in this case television news reporters) don't even know they misunderstand us. They honestly don't see their bias. That tells us, as Christians dealing with the secular media, that we need to exercise love in all of our contacts with them.

We should *not* be intimidated by them. They are in the darkness. We are in the light. We must respond from our position of light so that the darkened world can see what we see. We must never become defensive, angry, or rude as the world would have us become, because this would discredit our message. If ever there is a time to let the love of Jesus shine through us, it is when we speak to hundreds of thousands of viewers through television.

Given the reality of this problem—that Christians must deal with a sinful world that controls the most powerful method of communication ever devised by man—please let the suggestions in this book help you keep a proper perspective on your role as a Christian witness.

Summary

The problem is:
- Television news distorts reality in an effort to gain and hold our attention.
- Television news is controlled by worldly people and forces.
- Television news does not understand the light of the gospel.

---

[1]*Television Awareness Training: The Viewer's Guide for Family and Community,* edited by Ben Logan. Nashville: Abingdon, 1979, p. 156. Copyright by Media Action Research Center, Inc.
[2]Logan, ed., p. 156.

CHAPTER 2

The Medium

Television is a distinct medium of communication different from any other form of communication. The very fact that men put on makeup and read out loud while looking into a box full of electronic components points to the unnaturalness that TV speakers experience. Yet TV news anchors have learned certain techniques to present a more natural appearance to the viewer at home even though they are using an unnatural mode of communication.

The *Washington Journalism Review* recently published an article on the difficulties that print journalists have in making the transition from newspapers and magazines to television. The lessons learned and presented in this article serve as good beginning points for how we as Christians can learn to use television more effectively.

- Because television is a unique medium, prior experience in communication does not insure success in television.
- Pictures dominate the presentation of television news.
- To gain a natural appearance on television, one may

have to do some uncomfortable modifications in his presentation.
- Egos dominate the behind-the-scenes activities of television.

Reporters Have Wide Differences in Training

A few years ago, I conducted a survey of the prime news anchors of all three network affiliates in the top fifty cities of this country. This was for a paper I was writing on the effects of news consultants on television news. What I found was a less than uniform pattern for news anchors in their training, education, experience, insight and understanding of what television news reporting was about. Another survey of reporters done by Stephen Hess of the Brookings Institute in Washington, D.C. The conclusions are much the same, but Steve Hess has reached his more scientifically.

Hess's research is discussed in more detail in the next chapter.

Picture Scenes Dominate the News Story

Television news crews are so aware of the need for "good pictures" that they frequently present their stories according to how the video dictates. Charlene Canape, in the *Washington Journalism Review* article, "From Newsprint to Newscast" says, "The preoccupation with pictures dominates the news gathering process in TV. Even before a reporter does his reporting, he must know whom he wants to get on camera. Then the skilled reporter can produce more effective camera interviews."[1]

The necessity for vivid pictures is so overwhelming

that reporters put in and leave out portions of their stories depending upon what pictures they have. Often this lets extraneous factors dictate how the story is presented. Yet a realization of this fact can work to our advantage. Here's what I mean:

1. When your church or activity wants television coverage, be aware of the necessity of dramatic support

---

Case Study #1

Date: October 28, 1983
Location: Rochester, Minnesota
Principal: Dr. Francis Shaeffer
Brief Sketch of Events: While undergoing treatment for cancer at the Mayo Clinic, Dr. Francis Shaeffer led an anti-abortion demonstration at the Methodist Hospital in Rochester, which is connected to the clinic.

> Dr. Shaeffer attracted national attention to an issue that had already received a great deal of coverage—but that day, he made a special impact. He was able to contrast in a unique way his personal struggle for life with the death decision made by many mothers of the unborn. His own ability to choose life demonstrated that people want to live and suggested that if the unborn child had the choice, he or she would also choose to live.
> Try to present your point of view in a way that is new, unique, and visually dramatic. By "new and unique" I mean your presentation should be new to your TV viewership. It need not be universally new. Seek advice from leaders of similar organizations in other parts of the country. Be willing to experiment and to involve the active, creative minds of the young people in your organization.
> The best rule to follow is to seek or create those circumstances where your point of view will be most dramatically visualized. Don't worry about being overly dramatic. That rarely happens. And a decision to dramatize your ideas can always be "toned down" before it is presented to the press.

video for the news story. Help reporters along. Provide them with sources for support video. You might videotape people at a rally in support of your cause, for example, using colorful pictures showing banners, signs, slogans, and so forth. Think of other ways to visualize what you're talking about.

Consider the story of a church bus taking children to Sunday school. Provide the cameraman opportunity to ride on the bus, videotape the route, the children and the whole process of picking up kids. That is what the story is about; that is what will make it on the air. Be creative when it comes to providing sources of video for television news crews. This insures that *your* pictures get on the air, not the pictures they are forced to come up with when you don't provide them ways to "visualize your story."

2. Be selective in who speaks for your group. A good preacher is not always the best spokesperson for a TV interview. A mother who has children involved in a school prayer issue can probably speak more forcefully on that issue than the pastor of her church. Why? She is more directly affected! In the same way, the children involved may be able to speak more persuasively than their parents, because they are the ones affected.

Television news crews are always looking for the "real people" affected by the stories they cover. A way to insure your position gets on the air is to provide TV reporters with people affected by whatever is taking place. While these "real people" may not always replace the church spokesperson, they can be present to explain in "laymen's" language how a situation is affecting them directly. Let the pictures "tell" the story.

3. Overcommunicate with the reporter. Reporters do not know as much about the situation as you do. Whatever the story is, it is affecting the participants more than the reporter. You must be willing to instruct the

Case Study #2

Date: October 26, 1983
Location: Washington, D.C.
Principal: the wife of Alexander Solzhenitsyn
Brief Sketch of Events: The wife of Solzhenitsyn joined several congressmen on Capitol Hill in demanding that the United States State Department apply pressure to ease the persecution of Christians in Russia. The event attracted national coverage.

Mrs. Solzhenitsyn's presence added much to the rally. She was closer to the problem than any of the congressmen because of her husband's imprisonment in Russia. She was more qualified to talk about the problems because she knew of them firsthand. She brought to the rally an emotional involvement that added to the intrigue of the news coverage. She was a "representative figure" of the problem, allowing newsmen to visualize the grief, fear, uncertainty and turmoil that dissidents experience at the hands of the Soviet Union.

Your organization's point can be made effectively by such a spokesperson. Seek someone who has lived through the problem or been affected by the problem for which you have concern; for example, a teenage girl who has given birth rather than had an abortion. The spokesperson does not have to be a professional speaker.

Cover all aspects of the story. When presenting your story to the news media, touch on its legal, moral, practical, financial, and spiritual aspects. Church programs to house the poor, for example, involve many different considerations. Is the feeding of the poor in the church's facilities violating some local ordinance (as was the case of one church in Northern Virginia)? What is the cost involved in programs? And why does the church want to provide these benevolent services? You should have a person or persons who are qualified to speak about each aspect of the story available to answer questions. Have no more than one spokesperson per aspect of the story. There is no need to have two lawyers talking about the legal impact of the story, for example; one will do.

Limit the number of speakers to the few who can best

present your message with emphasis and simplicity. Rarely should you try to overwhelm the press with the large number of speakers you can gather.

Additional support people or spokespersons should be present only if they add to the impact of the presentation. You should include people who have met the qualifications of personal involvement and those who have "expert knowledge" of the topic as coming through academic expertise.

---

reporter in the best way to present the story. This subject is covered in more detail in another section of this guide. Be willing to help the reporter visualize the story, to point out what is the most effective way of letting the pictures tell the facts. Never become overbearing or condescending.

A Natural Appearance in an Unnatural Setting

In no other medium does the participant have to be more aware of every aspect of communication as that of television. He has to know how he looks, how his voice sounds, and how his gestures are adding to or detracting from the presentation of the message. He also must be aware of lights, cameras, settings, and other people who are important to the process, such as studio technicians and cameramen.

Television is a two-dimensional medium. The size and depth of the television screen limits the field of vision. Movements of hand or body forward or backward are minimized because of the compression of the image into a two-dimensional form. On the other hand, gestures from side to side that would appear perfectly normal in person may seem exaggerated on television.

I once had a talent coach from the Remyer-Gersin News Consulting Organization of Detroit give me the following tips on how to perform on television:

1. Gestures of body should be *more* dramatic when made forward. Gestures laterally should be more subdued because they may extend beyond the limits of the television screen.

2. Expressions of the face should be vivid and full of emotion. Virtually every expression appears more subdued on videotape than in real life. To compensate for this fact, facial expressions should take on added intensity, just as an actor on stage is more dramatic in that medium than when face-to-face with someone.

3. Projection of voice should be more controlled and sensitive to the demands of microphones. A speaker appears less intense when viewed on videotape. To make up for this, greater energy must be put into speaking, resulting in a more dramatic vocal presentation. You should speak loudly and clearly.

Virtually every television news reporter at one time or another has asked the person being interviewed to allow them to get videotape of the office setting with workers at their desks answering telephones and so forth. In those cases where the pictures must dominate the TV news story, be willing to "reenact" something for the cameras. This is not to say that we should "stage" the news, but by "role playing" for the cameras we can present a picture of a natural environment. Almost every time I have asked people to do that they express shyness. If coerced into doing the dramatization, they often appear stilted and uneasy because they don't feel comfortable on camera. How can this be overcome?

What you need to do as a church leader is to make those people present at the time of the interview aware of the fact that this "role playing" is a necessary part of the presentation of the story. Gain their enthusiastic cooperation before the TV crews arrive and tell them what they may be expected to do. This again allows you and your organization to have more control over what the viewers at home see and what impressions they are left with.

Also, the person being interviewed should be more conscious of his expressions and mannerisms. On TV, feelings of fear may be perceived as abruptness or hostility. If the church leader being interviewed is apprehensive on camera, that will be seen by the camera, and the audience at home will wonder why he is angry. From the beginning of the interview, you should be aware of the impression you are making and always present the facial and body expressions that will add to the story and not detract from it.

Stephen Aug of ABC News was asked about the extra attention he puts into his appearance when on TV. He explained the necessity of special grooming and attention to his attire this way: "If the main reason is so that your appearance doesn't detract from what you say—you don't want a viewer wondering what's with your nose rather than listening to your report—I'll do it."[2] Whatever is necessary to insure no detraction from the message or to insure an enhancement of the message ought to be done. We as Christian witnesses should be willing (as TV news reporters are willing) to do whatever is necessary to get the message out.

Speaking on television is not easy, but this should not be a cause for fear. Just as you have acquired skill at public speaking, you can acquire skill at television speaking. It may take some time. NBC Correspondent Ken Bode says, "Live TV can have the same effect as hanging ... in that it makes your eyes bulge."[3] Perhaps he has exaggerated, but you still have to put time into planning your television appearances or they won't go the way you want them to go.

Egos in the Newsroom

Egos dominate the news. This fact is rarely admitted, yet it is so true. When I was in the secular media, my colleagues could not see how their desires to be above everyone else affected their news judgment, their performance, their choice of jobs, their whole careers. I believed that TV journalists were led more by personal ambition and ego than by the salience of the stories they cover. I thought I had no way to prove my belief until I came upon two sources of information. One of them is the article I have cited from the *Washington Journalism Review*. The second is Stephen Hess's book, *The Washington Reporters*.

The *WJR* article quotes James Wooten as saying that "the added factor of ego . . . does presume itself in TV."[4] ABC newswoman Sheila Kast admits, "Even people who are good and know they are good get edgy when they haven't been on the air for a while."[5] This superficial observation does not indicate how ego demands of being on camera propel reporters into seeking the stories that will get them on the air. Reporters are looking for the unusual, the dramatic, the confrontational—in part because those occurrences tend to be defined as news, but also because the reporter who uncovers those stories will get his face on the air, the real "payoff" in television.

You may think I am being harsh to TV reporters. But I make this judgment on more than my personal experience of working with scores of them over many years. Hess's book tries to present an accurate, scholarly profile of reporters in Washington. In reference to television news reporters, he quotes an unnamed veteran TV reporter, who says, "Reporters are in a tizzy when their faces are not on the tube at least once every few days.'"[6] Hess outlines the average Washington reporter as a generalist who looks for excitement in an effort to avoid boredom. If Hess is correct about Washington reporters (and I believe the same conclusion can be reached of TV reporters nationwide), then this desire to experience excitement continually clouds their judgment of what is news and how it ought to be presented.

Egos *do* dominate TV news, but this can work to our advantage if we know how to deal with this fact. The bottom line for many reporters is "what makes me look good." With that tendency among TV reporters, let's give them what they want wherever possible.

Ways to Compensate for Ego Drive:
1. Be aware of the reporter's "bottom line" of needing to make a good report. This is his job, if not his whole life. Cooperation with him is essential to the story. If you serve as a "source" of information, he will rely on your knowledge to help him compete with any others who may be covering the story.
2. Assist the reporter wherever possible in securing necessary information on the story and praise him for the points he sees. Lead him through the material you want presented.
3. Present your situation in a way that will key into their desires to produce a good story. Emphasize the "newness" of the story you want presented, the ways in which this is a unique event or undertaking. The reporter must be given that sense of excitement they thrive upon. They must also be given the sense that this is new ground for them, that they are not just covering the same story for the fifteenth time. Make your interview with the reporter "come alive with excitement." If you do, you will get your material presented in a favorable way and you will give the reporters what they want. And *unless you give reporters what they want, you won't get what you want.*

---

[1]Charlene Canape, "From Newsprint to Newscast: The Great Reporter Crossover Is Not So Easy." *Washington Journalism Review*, October 1984, p. 33.
[2]WJR, p. 33.
[3]WJR, p. 33.
[4]WJR, p. 33.
[5]WJR, p. 33.
[6]Stephen Hess, *The Washington Reporters.* Washington, D.C.: The Brookings Institute, 1981, p. 121.

CHAPTER 3

The Messengers—TV Reporters

Television reporters and anchors hold a unique position in our society. They serve as "watchdogs" of what goes on in government and as disseminators of information to viewers. In essence, they keep us in touch with our world.

Problems arise because TV reporters, like the rest of us, carry prejudices. They cannot relate to their work and the subjects they cover in a completely objective way. Simply stated, reporters are human (and usually they are non-Christians).

Let's look at the traits of reporters to determine how we can best work with their limitations. The following profile of reporters is based upon thorough research of over one thousand reporters in the Washington, D.C. area done by Stephen Hess for his book, *The Washington Reporters.*

In my opinion, the listed traits are characteristic of television news reporters nationwide. Many of the Washington reporters have done service in smaller cities across the nation. The attractions to network television news are similar to those at the local level (prestige, travel, variety of assignments, etc.) and the training is also similar. In fact, if the assumption is made that some of the best reporters work in the nation's capital, reporters elsewhere may have even more glaring deficiencies than the ones Hess discovered. Bear in mind that Hess is a secular journalist reviewing secular journalists.

Specific Traits of Reporters

1. *Reporters want to be autonomous.*[1] This trait is tied directly with their sense of adventure, control, ego and freedom. They want to be in charge.

If reporters seek little guidance from their editors, then the persons we need to convince are the reporters themselves. When we convince reporters, we rarely have to worry about convincing their editors. Sometimes people try to go over the reporter's head to get a story aired. That almost always causes friction, which results in a negative story. Give the reporter room to operate and don't worry about persuading his whole news organization.

2. *Reporters frequently fail to research properly.*[2] The "wing it" attitude is prevalent in TV news. Why prepare? The interviewee will give all the answers. Hess said, "The research file of most reporters is a desk drawer of press clippings."[3] With this shallow understanding, the reporter may be ill-equipped to do the story.

If the minds of reporters are uncluttered by an understanding of the topic at hand, then it can be to our advantage to explain to them the essentials to this story. View this as an opportunity to instruct them about the topic in a "fresh" way.

3. *Reporters think of themselves as serious people.*[4] Regardless of their background reporters view themselves as professionals. In other words they rarely see

their faults. Reporters are people too, and Christians should not be intimidated by them. Yet they should be aware that reporters want to be treated as serious professionals, not unscholarly or frivolous.

4. *Reporters may subconsciously simplify events* as a way of limiting uncertainty and controlling their environment.[5]

Since reporters want to be in control, they seek to limit that which is out of their control or understanding. A story with many far-reaching ramifications may be simplified to the trite and superficial so the reporter can maintain control.

Christians can encourage a more favorable reporting of their viewpoints by careful presentation of the facts to reporters, so the reporter maintains better understanding of the issue.

5. *"Most reporters (in Washington) are liberal, college educated, male, white and middle class."*[6]

Christians should know they do face a liberally biased media virtually every time they are interviewed. Treat them with Christian love, yet caution.

6. *Reporters distrust public institutions and politicians.*[7]

While Hess's point here is about government, can anyone seriously question the media's distrust of organized religion as a public institution?

Christians should make every effort to convince reporters with facts and logical argument rather than emotional appeal (often used in sermons), which will invariably be discounted by a distrusting media. The burden of proof is upon the church in matters that are questioned.

7. *"Reporters are semiprofessionals and journalism could be characterized as a semiprofession."*[8] This

means there is no standard licensing procedure, no review board and no special course of study before entering in the job market.

Christians should consider reporters as information distributors who are skillful at disseminating material, but who are not necessarily skillful at interpreting material in some areas. Since religious matters are rarely a concern of reporters, they may be unfamiliar with matters of theology or portions of biblical text. Teach them as you would a beginning student of matters of the church and do so with love.

8. *Reporters seek scoops:* "The 'big' stories—the ones that win prizes—are often exposés."[9]

Christians should be aware that if there is a skeleton in the closet, a reporter will find it. God can forgive, but the press never forgives or forgets. Take the case of former Senator Roger Jepsen of Iowa. During the 1984 election campaign, he admitted he had filled out a registration form for a club that offered nude attendants. This occurred prior to this conversion, he said, but he still lost the election. It is best to "come clean" with information up front, rather than let a reporter uncover it at your most vulnerable moment.

9. *"The attraction of reporters to excitement biases news gathering."*[10]

Christians should seek to be genuine when dealing with reporters, but should be aware that excitement does trigger them into action. The tendency toward certain biases by reporters can be overcome with careful effort on the part of Christians. Present your Christian message creatively.

10. *"In an information system based on personal contacts, the affinity between reporters and sources helps shape the content of the news."*[11]

Case Study #3

Date: November 25, 1983
Location: a Maryland community
Principal: William Schul, a pro-life advocate
Brief Sketch of Events: Maryland officials confirmed reports that an abortion clinic had been dumping aborted fetuses at a local landfill since 1974. William Schul took the occasion to express hope that this practice would heighten alarm at the process of abortion. Most states disposed of aborted fetuses in less offensive ways. But even with a less offensive disposal of the fetuses, he said, abortion is wrong.

The weight of such evidence added to the claims that abortion is a brutal process. There was clearly no humanity involved in dumping these bodies in a landfill.

Schul's outrage was evidence of his personal conviction against abortion. More importantly it spoke to the reality that abortion is wrong, that it is a heartless atrocity and that victims are treated with disregard. Your response to your organization's concern should also express outrage where appropriate. You should show your emotions and demonstrate them with action, as Jesus did in clearing the temple of the moneychangers.

One of the keys to the effectiveness of Schul's statement was the timing. You should respond when the circumstances demand a response. Don't try to force the time and make a statement before you should. Be perceptive enough to know the most opportune moment, and continue to press the circumstances to help produce that moment.

The releasing of evidence by the state of Maryland gave Schul the most opportune moment to make his statements. Seek any form of "official" evidence that would be appropriate to your position: past court decisions, laws in other states, examples of the same problem in foreign countries and other evidence to add strength to your position. These sources of evidence should also carry emotional appeal—not to persuade reporters (use logic to do that), but for the TV audience, which can be persuaded with emotional appeal.

Christians can help themselves by helping the reporters. If affinity is useful with reporters, develop affinity. Refer to the suggestions on developing and maintaining media contacts later in this book.

11. *"There is a solipsistic (only the self) quality about reporters and politicians,* their sense that nothing can exist if it is not part of their own experience."[12]

Certainly in the area of religion, reporters are neophytes at best. They must be understood as being honestly ignorant of the workings of God, because they rarely chose to consider anything about Him.

12. *"Journalism is the only profession in which you can stay an adolescent all your life."*[13]

Journalism does not have the same opportunities for growth that many other professions do. A reporter may be a reporter thirty years. Another professional may have gone through several levels of management after thirty years, providing him with growth opportunities a reporter may not have.

A reporter may be frustrated by his lack of personal growth. This in turn may color his perceptions of life toward the negative.

13. *"The press always will be a reactive institution."*[14]

This is why we can't call a television station and simply say, "Our church is great, put us on the news." The press must react to some event, pseudo-event, or significant change in the status quo.

---

[1] Stephen Hess, *The Washington Reporters.* Washington, D.C.: The Brookings Institute, 1981, p. 5.
[2] Hess, page 18.
[3] Hess, page 21.
[4] Hess, page 21.
[5] Hess, page 21.

[6]Hess, page 67.
[7]Hess, page 78.
[8]Hess, page 82.
[9]Hess, page 88.
[10]Hess, page 125.
[11]Hess, page 126.
[12]Hess, page 126.
[13]Hess, page 128.
[14]Hess, page 130.

CHAPTER 4

Types of Interviews

While there are common factors among all kinds of interviews, certain traits are unique about each one. Here is a listing of the six major different types of interviews along with suggestions and a checklist for each.

The Office Interview

The reporter comes to your location and enters your environment. You have control of this setting, since you work in it each day. Presumably you knew the reporter was coming (unless it's *60 Minutes* with Mike Wallace knocking at your door). You should feel more at ease with interviews like these, in which you have time to prepare in advance and which take place in familiar surroundings. Treat the office interview as a conversation with a guest. Don't make it a test of wills.

Support people are vital for advance preparation. The best example here is the staff of U.S. Senator Jeremiah Denton of Alabama. I have a great deal of respect for Senator Denton because of his military career, his stance on moral issues and his unwavering friendliness. I am also impressed with his organized office.

Senator Denton's press secretary, Erna Engelkes, is always professional in dealing with the press. When I first approach the senator's office to set up an interview, she asks what questions I will ask the senator. I know

---

Case Study #4

Date: Fall 1983—Spring 1984
Location: Louisville, Nebraska
Principle: Pastor Everett Silevan
Brief Sketch of Events: Pastor Silevan of the Faith Christian School was arrested (literally from his pulpit) because of the question of teacher certification in the school and the school's continuation of an education program despite the state of Nebraska's orders against continuation.

By allowing television news crews into the church to videotape the arrest of the pastor, Silevan brought a vivid picture before many television viewers. As one news report indicated, people were seeing "what they never thought would happen in the United States—a pastor being led away to jail for his religious beliefs." The media can serve to present our message to millions of people. It can show abuse of religious freedoms as well as the abuse of other freedoms. In today's world churches need the media to help present their messages.

Here it is not our place to judge whether the pastor was correct in defying the state's orders. One must consider the leading of the Holy Spirit in the matter. From a communications aspect, however, Silevan did what would most effectively visualize the story. He insisted that the law enforcement officers arrest him from his pulpit and he allowed himself to be led away by officers of the law to jail. No number of newspaper, magazine or radio reports could present this story with the same impact as one TV news story showing the pastor being led away. Television can serve as a magnifying glass to present the conflict between groups. Seek ways to have television news present the contrast between your organization's position and that of your opposition.

If you have the option of deciding where the conflict will

be recorded by the news media, you have three general places to choose from—"your turf," "their turf," or "neutral turf."

1. *Your turf.* Pastor Silevan made his impact in part because his turf was being "invaded." He had no other choice but to allow TV news crews record the process of his arrest. As a general rule seek news coverage on some location other than your turf, unless that is part of the story as it was in Silevan's case. You should show conflict on your turf only when it has been invaded. Churches are sanctuaries of peace. Discord at these places should be presented only when some outsider has come into your organization on the attack.

2. *Their turf.* If your group is maintaining the proper position in the controversy and the other group is at fault, then in terms of communication it would be natural for the conflict to be played out on their turf.

Being on their turf gives them certain communication advantages, however. By going on their turf, you become the "invader."

3. *Neutral turf.* Both groups are on equal footing, yet neutral turf may not be the best location to present conflict.

Consider the choice of conflict locations as a military expert chooses the places of battle. Each case must be taken separately. Choose the location that

- Gives your organization the greatest position of strength
- Lessens the number of weakness
- Enhances the message

---

that by giving her the questions beforehand, the senator will have answers prepared, which will make his job and mine easier.

During the interview his staff sits in the office and is ready to provide additional documents that may be needed or to be sent on information searches that may come up unexpectedly. Does this take away from the interview process? Not in the least—it does the opposite. The senator's office is assured of presenting factual information and I am assured of getting all the information I need for the story I am doing.

When church leaders are interviewed, they should do the same things: have the staff screen the reporters for questions, have necessary information readily at hand and be present during the interview to catch anything that is not said the way you want it presented. No one is flawless. It is always wise to have a safeguard.

Office Interview Checklist:
Pre-Interview
____ Find out the names of the reporter and his crew and give them to your receptionist.
____ Determine what subjects will be discussed (when possible, get the specific questions in advance).
____ Determine the time and place for the interview.
____ Arrange to meet any technical needs the reporting team may have (such as an extension cord or other electrical needs).
____ Have your staff brief you on the latest developments; brief them on the nature of the interview and ask them to be present during the interview.
____ Prepare an information kit for the reporting team: facts about your organization, your personal background, and the latest information on the topic to be reviewed in the interview.
____ Where practical arrange to have coffee or soft drinks for the reporting team.
____ Seek God's guidance for the right attitude, preparation, and delivery for the interview process. Do this alone and with your staff as well.

Office Interview Checklist:
Time-of-Interview
____ Re-instruct your receptionist to be friendly and to use the reporters' names.
____ Be courteous yourself, as if entertaining guests.
____ Remain calm and prayerful.
____ Answer only what the reporter asks. Use the tech-

niques discussed earlier on answering questions and leading the conversation toward your goals.
____ Follow suggestions on controlling your delivery (p. 67).
____ Start your answer over again when necessary.
____ Work with a brief time frame (20 to 30 seconds per answer).
____ Following the interview, ask the reporter if he needs any additional information.
____ Ask the reporter to call you if he has any additional questions, and tell him you will call him back if there are any new developments.

Office Interview Checklist:
Post-Interview
____ Write a thank-you note to the reporter.
____ State again your willingness to answer any additional questions.
____ When appropriate write the station's news director a favorable note on the reporter's performance.
____ Review the interview with staff who were present. Determine the areas where the interview went well and where it could have gone better.
____ List possible causes of the weakness of the interview and ways to improve your interview techniques. Select one way to improve and begin working on that area.
____ Alert your organization members of the time the story will air and seek their input afterward. Review their suggestions with your staff, and use them as ideas for improvement.

The Press Conference Interview

The press conference differs from the other types of interviews. The dynamics include more than one reporter and frequently more than one person responding to the questions.

Few press conferences take into consideration the appearance of the room as it will look on camera. To the natural eye a room may appear to be neat and orderly, but on camera the room may change its appearance because of the "flattening" of the image. The human eye sees life in three dimensions. The eye of the camera "sees" things in two dimensions.

Problems for cameramen arise at press conferences when the panel of speakers is too close to the wall and there is insufficient room to provide back lighting to the people. When the table or lectern is only a few feet from the wall, then the lights in front of the person on camera throw his shadow onto the wall behind him. The moving shadow on the wall behind the speaker is more than just annoying; often the features of the speaker are distorted, making him appear comical.

When setting up a press conference, attention should also be paid to the color of the wall behind the speaker. Walls with flesh-colored paint should be avoided, because the face of the speaker could get lost in the background. (Even on the national and international levels little attention is given to the proper setting for a press conferences. The press room at the U.S. State Department has a flesh-colored map behind the speakers, and faces can appear to be grotesque by the blending of features of the face with jagged features on the map.) Backdrops of floral wallpaper, odd designs, and doors should be avoided. Above all, any items behind the speaker should not appear to be "growing" out of his head. A simple but necessary question to the cameraman will prompt him to check for extraneous items that should be moved before taping begins.

Whenever possible a panel of speakers should have individual microphones in front of them. These individual microphones should then be wired to a "mult" box from which camera crews can plug in. This centralized wiring will avoid a cluster of microphones at a lectern and having the speakers get up from their chairs to move to the lectern. (When this happens, the speaker often begins answering the reporter's question as he is walking to the microphone and the first part of his answer is lost.) The individual microphone in front of each speaker will insure that any response is carried immediately. It is also far easier for the professional cameraman to pivot the camera and move from speaker to speaker than it is for the speaker to move to the lectern.

The room should be just large enough to accommodate the anticipated number of reporters, guests, and television crews. A larger room than necessary creates a dull atmosphere; a smaller room than necessary creates too much tension. The desirable atmosphere is one where there is the anticipation of something important.

Camera crews should be centralized on a platform in the back of the room.

The length of the conference will determine whether seating will be provided for reporters.

Press Conference Checklist:
Pre-Conference List

____ With staff, determine what issues need to be addressed at the press conference.

____ Prepare materials to be given to the press, including background information on your organization, yourself and other participants, and on the topic(s) to be discussed.

____ Call the members of the press and invite them to the conference. Invite them only after you know what you're going to say to them.

____ Ask them for firm commitments to come. Tally the number expected. Arrange for the room to accommodate only the number coming.

____ Arrange for refreshments for those who are coming (coffee, tea, juice or soft drinks, and pastries or other snacks, depending on the time of day).

___ Determine ways your group can demonstrate your ideas, visualize your concerns or communicate your point of view.
___ Follow up the written notice of with press conference with a telephone invitation the day before.
___ Review with staff the points to be presented.
___ When possible do a "dry run" of the conference. Deliver your address and ask for questions from an audience assembled from staff members. Stick to your schedule—coach each speaker in advance not to run long.
___ Seek media advice when necessary from a professional press agency or public relations firm.

Press Conference Checklist:
During the Press Conference
___ Begin on time and stick to your schedule.
___ Prepare a way for latecomers to take their seats that will not interfere with camera angles.
___ Establish the ground rules in your opening statements:
- How you want to answer questions (after each speaker or after all prepared statements)
- Limits on the number of questions for each speaker or on each subject
- How you want to introduce speakers (all at once or before each speaker)
- Once you have outlined these rules, be sure to adhere to them. Allow no exceptions!

___ Use charts, graphs and other visual aids. These should be duplicated in press kit for each reporter. You should also indicate that cameramen will have access to the visuals *after* the press conference is over.
___ Maintain control of the presentation and the question/answer period. One way to keep in control is to have each reporter stand and give his or her name and company before asking a question.

_____ Allow questions to come naturally, but control their direction by the responses you give.

_____ Close the question/answer period by saying, "We'll take one or two more questions." Try to conclude the conference with the answer to a *positive* question. If you receive a negative question, depending on how negative it is, you may want to take another question. If that one is positive, you will end on an "up" note. If both the final questions are negative, it is definitely time to end the conference!

Press Conference Checklist:
Post-Conference List
Immediately after the conference

_____ Have someone assist the camera people in getting the videotape of the visuals you produced.

_____ Have staff members seek out reporters and their questions. Don't wait for them to seek you out. They may not do so and may leave the conference with wrong ideas. Anticipate any additional questions the reporters may have.

_____ Have the speakers meet the members of the press. Regardless of how smoothly the conference ran have the speakers greet the press and react with them warmly. Fences have been mended during these times and warm relations made warmer.

Within twenty-four hours of the press conference

_____ Preferably as soon after as possible, follow up the information to the reporters with a phone call to their newsroom. Ask if there are any questions and offer any other assistance.

_____ Review the event with your staff:
- What worked well?
- What needs improvement?
- What caused the problems?
- What can be done to make improvements before the next press conference?

- How can your organization be more effective in disseminating the information you want distributed to the press?

____ Determine the reactions from the reporters:
- Which were most supportive?
- Which were most negative?
- What were the major points of concern from the negative reporters?
- What can be done to "win them over"?
- What steps will you take within twenty-four hours to accomplish the goal of winning the negative reporters to your way of thinking?

____ Expect *all* of the reporters present at your conference to have some doubts about your presentation. Never criticize them for minor errors. Correct major errors, but do it carefully.

The Event Interview

An event interview occurs unexpectedly when you are at the scene of an event that has just taken place. For example, there is a fire on the church premises and you have to respond quickly to questions from news reporters. Keep calm. Despite the rush of emotions and flurry of activity, respond to the reporters' questions honestly and succinctly.

Event Interview Checklist:
Pre-Event
There is no way to prepare in a specific sense for some unknown tragedy, accident, benevolent award, or other unexpected occurrence. Two general items to check are:

____ Be in good stead with God—run a tip-top operation for His glory. Never cut corners!

____ Know as much about your operation as possible. What you don't know, have staff members who do.

Event Interview Checklist:
During the Interview
____ Be calm.
____ Be optimistic and hopeful.
____ Be insightful.
____ Be brief.

Event Interview Checklist:
Post-Interview
____ Watch the news story featuring your interview and determine ways you could have improved it.
____ Ask friends to watch and get their advice on how to improve.

The Pseudo-Event Interview

A pseudo-event is a "staged event" interview, planned in advance. Pseudo-events include rallies, marches, demonstrations, and so forth. They differ from planned office interviews because the environment of the pseudo-event changes the dynamics of the interview process. They differ from event interviews because you have time to prepare for a reporter's questions.

Always allow the activity of the pseudo-event to serve as a background during the interview. If the sound of the activities can be picked up by the interview microphone, so much the better. Try not to let the reporter interview you in a quiet place. That defeats the purpose of the pseudo-event setting.

The Pseudo-Event Checklist:
Pre-Pseudo-Event
____ Plan the activities to be presented during the pseudo-event (such as marches, speeches, rallies, etc.) The most effective pseudo-event will be one that best presents the concerns of your organization in a *visual* way.

____ In the same manner as a press conference, determine which members of the press are coming and how many. (Refer to Press Conference checklist, p. 40, for appropriate items).

The Pseudo-Event Checklist:
During the Pseudo-Event
____ Stick to your schedule.
____ Have staff members seek out reporters during the pseudo-event to answer their questions and to make sure the reporters are not confused on any points.
____ Staff members should also find out how the pseudo-event is being perceived by the reporters. They should not ask overtly, but through other

---

Case Study #5

Date: November 24, 1983
Location: Cincinnati, Ohio
Principal: Jerry Kirk, Senior Pastor at College Hill Presbyterian Church
Brief Sketch of Events: Pastor Kirk gathered other ministers and concerned individuals at a meeting to present to the nation the destructive effects of pornography. He and the other individuals called their group Citizens Concerned for Community Values. He held a three-day convention on fighting pornography and called upon President Reagan to join the battle. Media coverage was primarily local.

   There is strength in numbers—even greater strength when the numbers reflect diversity in the congregations represented. This approach by Pastor Kirk insured a large base of support. It multiplied the number of people who would be spreading the message of the coalition and thus the number of people who would be interested in watching any television reports concerning its activities.

Pastor Kirk chose a positive rather than a negative name for his group. It is important to keep in mind that as Christian speakers our task is not only to speak against sin, but to speak for righteousness. Pastor Kirk wanted everyone to know he was for righteousness more than being against anything.

Seek as broad a base of support and involvement as possible. Stop short, however, of compromises that render your message meaningless or ineffective. "Sell" your ideas to other leaders in your community for their support. In doing so you must give them some reasons why their participation in your project would be beneficial to them. There must be some practical reasons for other groups to help your organization. Remember, "It's amazing what someone can accomplish if he doesn't care who gets the credit." Share the credit with the other groups who join in your project.

A rally might support your cause in the following ways:

1. *Media attention.* Media can find several spokespersons at one location. Media have more opportunities to do reports during the week.

2. *Collective thought.* New ideas and methods are presented when creative thinkers get together.

3. *Absorption time.* Media and audiences will have more time to understand your organization and its goals.

---

questions: "Will the activities today help you visualize your story better?" Or, "What aspect of the story will you use in the beginning of your report?" Be careful in the questioning. Reporters should not feel you're trying to tell them what to write or report.

The Pseudo-Event Checklist:
Post Pseudo-Event

_____ Maintain the same contact with reporters as described under the Press Conference checklist.

_____ Conduct the same post-analysis of the pseudo-event as described under the Press Conference checklist.

_____ Was the pseudo-event understood as a means of visualizing the concerns your group has?

_____ How was it perceived? Was it *too* theatrical?
_____ What follow-up can you and staff do to enhance relations with the press who attended the pseudo-event?
_____ What other ways can your group demonstrate your ideas, visualize your concerns, or communicate your point of view?

The Stakeout Interview

This occurs when reporters are hoping to get an interview—quick in nature—as the interviewee exits a courtroom, walks down a hallway, or enters or leaves a car. These should be treated as a pseudo-event interview—you are somewhat prepared for what they are going to ask you, yet the environment is an unfamiliar one.

Unless you are well-prepared for these interviews, avoid them. They are places where you can say damaging information when put under so much pressure. Stakeout interviews are completely to the reporter's advantage and rarely will they serve the purpose of the interviewee. Avoid them whenever possible.

The Stakeout Interview Checklist:
Pre-Interview
_____ You should anticipate that reporters are awaiting your appearance and will want to discuss the issue on your departure from the courthouse, conference room, or other meeting. Have your staff so well-trained that they can get word to you in advance about a stakeout interview.

The Stakeout Interview Checklist:
During the Interview
_____ Be brief.
_____ Be honest.
_____ Be factual.

_____ Invite the press to a press conference within a reasonable time after the stakeout interview. Never expect to give all answers at a stakeout interview.

The Stakeout Interview Checklist: Post-Interview
_____ Prepare for the press conference (refer to the Press Conference checklists)

The Talk Show Interview

Here are some special concerns. In addition to treating this type of interview as a conversation with a friend, you must also be aware that thousands—in some cases, millions—of other "friends" are watching on television. You must also be aware of the lights, floor personnel, and so forth.

Frequently, people going on talk shows are hit with an unexpected format that throws them off guard. They become uneasy and leave their best image at home. They come away feeling disappointed about themselves and their appearance.

Frequently as well, reporters or talk show hosts fail to reveal certain aspects about their programs in an effort to gain the upper hand. When a guest is uneasy, the host is more in control. It is always the obligation of the guest to find out the format of the program he will appear on.

Differences are noticeable from newscast to newscast and talk show to talk show. Do the anchors on a news program want the guest to appear with them on the news set? Or does one of the anchors leave the news desk and take a seat in a more relaxed setting for the interview portion of the programs? Do talk show hosts want to engage in conversation with their guests or conduct a formal interview with structured questions and answers?

There is no single answer to how you should conduct

yourself while doing a live television interview. There is a single answer to what you should do before the interview takes place: know as much as possible about the program and the host before you appear on the show. Know the format. Know the interviewer's usual line of questioning. Know if he has prejudices and weaknesses. Know your interviewer as you would the opposing side in a debate. A great strength in an interview is to know the probable reaction by the interviewer to what you say.

Briefly meet the host before the program starts, confess any nervousness which you may have and ask for his help. He's in his comfortable environment. He will want to make the show a success and more often than not will offer to give you any assistance you need to "get through the interview." If you approach it the opposite way—that you can take on the world—his attitude will most likely be to knock you off your pedestal. *You need him. He* needs *you at your best.* He will want to help you reach your best.

After discussing these concerns with him, offer him a level of trust, but keep a reserve control within yourself. Don't let him orchestrate you completely. If you do, you'll be manipulated into his control even more until you say something you regret. Also, be on guard for the unexpected question. As soon as the host thinks he can spring something on you, he will do so. Take the needed guidance until you have acclimated to the TV studio's environment. Then command his attention and the attention of your audience by what you say. Follow the Trojan horse tactic. Get into his camp unnoticed, then when you can, go on the aggressive with the points you need to make.

Talk Show Interview Checklist:
Pre-Interview

_____ Learn as much as you can about the program you're going to appear on, the network or station

that carries the program, and the issue to be discussed.
___ Talk to other people who have appeared on this program. Get their impression of the host(s) and the format.
___ Arrive early.
___ Talk to the host(s) before the program starts.

Talk Show Interview Checklist:
During the Interview
___ Remain prayerful.
___ Remain calm.
___ Seek assistance from the program host(s).
___ Lead the host with your answers to the conclusions you want him, the studio audience, and the viewers to reach.
___ Watch for time cues—not those to the host, only those to you. Follow them precisely.

Talk Show Interview Checklist:
Post-Interview
___ Follow up each appearance with a thank-you note to the host(s), the producer, the station manager, and others who were instrumental in the program
___ Seek reactions from your staff, organization members, and "third party" sources on what you did well and what you can do to improve your TV appearances in the future.

CHAPTER 5

Interview Problems and Needs

Openness During the Interview

Reporters smell blood from wounds the way sharks sense an injured swimmer. The way to prevent this is to go into an interview "unwounded." There can be no indication that you are trying to hide anything or reporters will focus on that aspect and forget everything else. Reporters need something to keep them from being bored. One of the surest ways to do that is to hide something, give only part of the truth, or indicate there is an area about the subject under question you do not wish to discuss. If you're not open, you pay the price of losing control and losing the cooperation of the reporter. You will also lose on the issue of trustworthiness.

I saw a clear example of the effects of not being open while I was in the Midwest. A group of ministers had come together to fight pornography. They called a press conference and were ready to present staggering information on the extensive use of pornography by our society and the detrimental effects it has. One prominent opponent of media smut was asked to answer a question pertinent to the question at hand. He said, "No comment." A follow-up question from the reporter was,

"Why don't you want to answer?" The minister said, "No big deal, I just don't."

The reporter was obviously affronted and that offense affected how he did his story. Reporters are human; they react as humans. The minister should not have been at a press conference if he did not want to answer questions.

The reason the minister did not want to answer the reporter's question was his general distrust of the media and his view that they are all misguided sinners. While I may agree with his thesis that the bulk of reporters are liberal in their perspectives and are unaware of the gospel, they still must be treated with respect and love, not antagonism.

When we let our fear, apprehensions, and distrust affect how we present the message of Christ (even to worldly people) then we are an obstacle to the gospel. Be open to reporters and willing to explain to them anything they want to know.

Makeup for the Interview

The use of makeup for television interviews is an option you should consider. For interviews of the stakeout, event, or private nature, there is less need for it. But if the interview will be done in a television studio, you should expect to have a makeup artist prepare you for the cameras.

If you do not know whether or not the television station has a professional makeup artist, you should bring an assortment of makeup items. Basic to the preparation for on-camera/studio interviewing is a pancake powder (Max Factor Tan 1 or Tan 2 works well). If you have a heavy beard (shadow), a cream-colored "beard cover" makeup should be applied to the face before the darker tan base is used. The beard cover makeup (which can either be a white or flesh-colored powder or oil base cream) can also be used to "fill in" lines or shadows on the face. Finally, you may need a darker pancake or cream for highlighter.

The procedure for being "made up" for a studio interview should follow this general plan:

1. A beard cover of a light flesh-colored cream should be applied first.

2. The medium-dark Tan 1 or Tan 2 pancake base should be applied next.

3. Any lines, wrinkles, or shadows should be filled in and blended with the pancake base until the skin appears smooth.

4. Broad features of the face (primarily the nose) can be made to appear more narrow on camera by applying a dark cream to the thumb and forefinger then following the bridge of the nose downward. This darker makeup should be applied lightly and then blended with the other makeup. This can also make slight deviations in the nose vanish and the nose will appear more straight and narrow.

5. The final touch to makeup application is a check to see all makeup is blended together and a check to see if the lights from the makeup mirror do not make your face shine. If a shine occurs, then a brushing of flesh-colored powder will dull the gloss from the makeup cream and resulting appearance on camera will be normal to the eyes of the viewers at home.

Anticipating Reporters' Questions

Most reporters are ill-prepared or at best are shallow in their understanding of the subject. Stephen Hess in *The Washington Reporters* says reporters in Washington D.C. suffer from being generalists.[1] Their specialties (if they have any) may not allow them the kind of in-depth knowledge of a subject that they should have. Since reporters are not thorough in preparing for a story, as Hess suggests, then you need to do the preparation for the reporters.

Fundamental journalism still looks at six questions: Who, What, When, Where, How, and Why. These basic questions can be anticipated easily. Other questions are for more clarification of these broad questions.

You should keep in mind these ideas in anticipating the questions reporters are most likely to ask.

1. *How does this event* (situation, law, ruling, etc.) *affect the masses of people?* Have specific answers. Quote facts and figures on impact.

2. *Why are you personally involved in this subject?* Here is an opportunity for the reporter to gain insight into what compels you as a church leader to take a stand on some subject. Are you hiding secrets? If you are, don't get involved. Reporters always look for ulterior motives.

3. *What's in it for you?* Similar to number two, but more specific about any ulterior motive.

4. *What happens if the status quo is allowed to continue?* For example, abortion is allowed and society continues on. Why change the law now?

5. *What will be the financial cost if we do what you want us to do?* When appropriate, this question can trigger an acquired response from reporters. They can see a firm way of defining impact and have a better understanding of how the story affects people.

Have a fellow worker quiz you on your knowledge of the story before the interview takes place. Brainstorm on the possible approaches a reporter may take in looking at the information you want presented. As in a public speaking situation, the one who knows forty times as much about his subject than is needed is the one who will come across as the most at ease.

---

[1]Stephen Hess, *The Washington Reporters.* Washington, D.C.: The Brookings Institute, 1981, p. 122.

CHAPTER 6

Personal Tips Before You Go On

The following suggestions will enhance your effectiveness while on TV.

Be Unique

TV news reporters want to cover exciting stories. They live for the next unique event. Unless you have something that is different than what has been seen on television countless times already, you can forget about appearing on the tube. Every day newsrooms must decide what is news and what is not. A news director in a medium-sized city once told me that the best definition he knew was, "News is what I say it is." Such an arbitrary and subjective way of deciding what is presented on the air is not always fair, but it is the way news judgments are made.

Reverend John Burns of the Rock Assembly of God in Lima, Ohio was fighting pornography, and he gained national attention for the way he did so. The deeply committed pastor carried a cross as he walked the eighty-three miles from Toledo to Lima to dramatize his burden for those caught in pornography and to gain support against the trend toward more adult bookstores and prostitution in his town. Reverend Burns was more successful in attracting attention with his July through August, 1983 march than if he had merely held a press conference and railed against indecency. Because he had been willing to undergo the hardship of bearing the cross, Burns demonstrated his heartfelt concern, his commitment to solving the problem, and his love for those caught in the grasp of sexual sins. He demonstrated his love in a unique way—one in which no one could deny his sincerity.

In dealing with the press, be unique.

Be Brief

The constraints of television dictate that news reports are weighed in seconds. A long network story is two minutes, or 120 seconds. An average local story may be one and a half minutes, or ninety seconds. When the reporter's narrative is considered and the probability of an interview on the "opposing side" is taken into account, you can see that an excerpt from your interview can run no more than fifteen to twenty-five seconds.

Speak in concise, brief statements. Make each answer to each question a unit. Don't drag on the answer and take this as an opportunity to give all your "good stuff" in one outburst. More questions will follow. You'll get your chance to say what you want to say.

By making the answers shorter several beneficial results will occur.

1. You maintain better control of what you say and there will be less likelihood of making a misstatement.

2. The reporter will be forced to work more; he will have to ask more questions. By getting him more involved in the process and answering the specific questions he has in his mind at the moment, you will be less likely to confuse him or lose him in your line of thinking.

3. The primary reason for brief answers is found in

the control you have over what is used on the air. By giving simple, short answers you almost insure that your full answer to one of the reporter's questions will be used in a story, rather than having him abruptly cut you off in the middle of your major point.

In answering reporters' questions, be brief.

Be Informed

Working at the Christian Broadcasting Network has enabled me to see top-notch information gathering and funneling to the proper people. Every story that airs on the 700 Club carries with it an information sheet for the host, Pat Robertson, to review. Pat is an extremely well-read individual. Yet he takes that additional step of being informed about the specifics of the five-minute story to be presented on the air that day. Many times he could "from the cuff" deliver a half-hour lecture on the topic without notes, to the audience's amazement. Yet he still want a "backgrounder" before the story airs.

Dr. Paul Craig Roberts, the cornerstone architect of "Reaganomics," appears regularly on the 700 Club as an expert economist. He is exactly that. One morning it was my pleasure to escort Dr. Roberts into the studio for that morning's live broadcast from Washington to the rest of the nation. Dr. Roberts firmly but politely insisted on seeing a copy of that morning's newspaper before being interviewed. Here is a man who has a Ph.D. in economics, writes regular articles, and receives regular briefings from government staff and officials. Yet he would not have appeared on our program until he had a chance to see if the newspaper contained anything he needed to know. Why?

Clearly both Dr. Robertson and Dr. Roberts have the professionalism to be fully prepared. Neither wants to be vulnerable at any point, for when vulnerability is present, reporters will find it.

The lesson to us is clear—prepare for an interview in such a way that you are informed about any new developments in the subject to be discussed.

Case Study #6

Date: September 27, 1983
Location: northeastern Tennessee
Principal: Reverend Richard Taylor (no relation)
Brief Sketch of Events: The local cable TV company began carrying the Playboy Channel. Taylor polled citizens in that part of the state to ascertain if they wanted the channel in their community. The results may have been useful in determining if the community standards had been violated as laid out by the U.S. Supreme Court.

The strength of what Pastor Taylor had to say against the Playboy Channel was found in the poll he took. He was not speaking just for himself, but for the whole community. As a general rule, news media will not respond to just another poll or just another petition against something. But when a poll or petition can be used to show overwhelming opposition to an immoral activity, then its use is recommended.

The U.S. Supreme Court has decided that communities have the final say in what they view as moral and immoral. That is true in theory. There may be some cases falling on either side of that line—where community standards have been abused or upheld by that guideline. Regardless, it is always better to have as much evidence against such pornography as possible. Using the poll as evidence of community standards was a useful attempt to show opposition to the Playboy Channel.

Legal precedent can also be used as evidence. The key to applying a legal precedent is finding one that closely parallels your current situation or speaks directly to the point in question. Keep the prior cases you select meaningful. The news media will not respond to even a mountain of references that do not address the heart of the matter—but they will listen to one concise, pertinent case.

Be Honest

Cincinnati Gas and Electric was one of the companies building a nuclear power plant in Ohio. Once completed the Zimmer nuclear power plant was to supply a sufficient amount of electricity for the southwest Ohio area at a reasonable cost.

In addition to the concerns about nuclear power in the wake of the Three Mile Island incident in Pennsylvania, questions were raised about the cost of the plant. Initially, C.G.&E. was able to address these concerns with facts and figures. The press reported the story of the plant in an accurate way.

During the time of construction, delays became the norm and cost overruns became customary. News reports began to increase about the inefficiency of the construction team and the additional burdens the customers of C.G.&E. would have to pay for the cost overruns. The tide began to turn against the Zimmer plant and against C.G.&E.

More dramatic revelations followed. Excesses were discovered in wages. The quality of materials used was below government standards. A general feeling existed that Zimmer was poorly constructing the plant.

Officials of C.G.&E. were perceived as covering up something or even lying about what was and was not done at the Zimmer plant. The press went on the attack. Reports raising more questions were broadcast and the end result of the whole process was that the Zimmer project was shut down. Today the empty plant stands as a reminder of what poor press relations can do to the image of a company.

Failure to tell the whole truth and nothing but the truth can adversely affect a minister or a church. I have used a secular example for the topic of honesty, but we should be even more aware that we must always present the truth.

Be Helpful

There are three ways you can help the reporting team that comes to interview you. The first is in the area of physically getting the interview done. Help the technicians with any electrical needs they may have. They may need one or two extension cords or additional lighting. Perhaps you might even keep a small tool kit handy.

Another way you can help the reporter is by understanding the material you want to present. Speak in laymen's language about the issue. Suggest additional people for the reporter to interview or other sources of information to which he can refer for a better understanding. Help him in any way that you can to do the report.

A third way to help the reporter is to tell the reporter you will be available for additional calls he may need to make to you after he gets back to the station. Frequently, between the early evening news and the late evening news, a station wants a reporter to get a "fresh lead" to the story. Offer to meet the reporter between shows if that is appropriate. Offer to contact him the next day. Don't give him the impression you are second-guessing him or wanting to review his work; make it clear that you just want to be available if he wants another interview. It will work to your advantage if you establish a good rapport with the reporter.

Be Hospitable

Reporters prefer to be treated as honored guests. This may mean some extra effort on your part or on the part of your church to show hospitality to visiting reporters. Start from the beginning contact. Indicate an eagerness to discuss with the reporter whatever topic he wants to feature in a report, even if it is a negative one. Don't indicate any reluctance to be interviewed.

Once a time has been arranged for the reporter to come to your office, tell your receptionist to expect the interviewer, his cameraperson, and an additional technician or two. Get the names of as many of these people as possible. Always get the name of the reporter who will do the interview. Instruct the receptionist to use the reporter's name when greeting him.

In nearly ten years of reporting I have been greeted this way only once. It was when I interviewed a spokesman for the Independent Sector about the Treasury Department's proposal to tax charitable contributions. Can you imagine the shock and delight I had when for the first time in ten years, a receptionist not only knew I was coming, but who I wanted to see and even my name? It really picked me up. If you use this little step in greeting your reporter, it will help your situation also.

When the reporter and the crew come into your office, offer them coffee, tea, or a soft drink. If you are holding a press conference, you will want to serve coffee and donuts or other pastries. These are nice gestures on your part, which are appreciated by the media.

Throughout the time the reporting team is with you, treat them as guests whom you are pleased to see. Even if they become offensive, display hospitality. In fact, your hospitality will dissuade many reporters from being rude. It won't always work, but it will help.

Be Insightful

Viewers at home always watch for the "realness" of ministers. Are professing Christians genuine in their faith? Do they live by Christian principles? Nothing heightens the potential to make a favorable or a negative impression than a television interview in the midst of a crisis. Will the Christian "break" under the circumstances of the moment? Crises are great times to see what is really inside of us. The Christian writer Oswald

Chambers said, "Our private life is disciplined by the interference of people in our own matters."[1]

One of the best ways for you to remain calm and spiritual during such an "interference" by a news reporter (especially when being interviewed on television about the crisis) is to look for some spiritual insight into what is taking place. What is God saying to you through the crisis? How will the crisis affect your church? What does God say to men through any crisis? Times of turmoil are times to speak about God's sovereign control, His eternal plan, His ability to work through circumstances, and His limitless ability to restore that which has been destroyed by sin, tragedy, or mismanagement. Seek those insightful aspects of the crisis upon which you are asked to reflect and you will convey the message of God to the television audience, even during the most trying of situations.

The insights you reach should be shared with the TV audience fully. Nonbelievers can relate to real Christians dealing with real circumstances. Your insightful "realism" may prove beneficial to some nonbeliever in making a decision for the Lord. Your covering up or glossing over tragedy in a way that shows shallowness or "phoniness" will hinder the message of God to someone who wants a way to deal with real tragedy in his or her life. True spiritual insight will show the nonbeliever that Christians have comfort even in tragedy. When in the midst of a TV interview concerning a tragedy, seek spiritual insights.

Be Optimistic and Hopeful

In keeping with what we have just discussed—spiritual insight in the midst of crisis—the Christian being interviewed on TV during the aftermath of a tragedy should look to hope for the future. The world has no hope in dealing with tragedy, only the continued expec-

Case Study #7

Date: December 15, 1983
Location: Portsmouth, New Hampshire
Principal: Pastor Wayne Price
Brief Sketch of Events: In mid-December of 1983, vandals torched a nativity scene built by his church. Afterwards, Reverend Price reacted to the destruction by pointing out the broad support the church had received to rebuild the scene. Many people had sent money to the church for the rebuilding effort.

Recalling the battles of Israel in the Old Testament, it was often customary to count the size of the opposition. Here, Pastor Price wanted to show that those standing for the right were many in number. He showed the opposition the extent to which the support for the nativity scene was real in the community of Portsmouth.

In a case like this one, a reaction of anger can refute our claims of being Christlike. Reactions of sadness and misunderstanding can heighten the awareness a community feels for the atrocities committed. When forgiveness is mixed with the sadness, then the Christian group can speak against the violence and the viewers will listen.

You do not need to "sugarcoat" sin or wrongdoing, but try to offer more than just a condemnation. Seek the positive aspects of your church's involvement in some community disagreement. The more you do so, the more your opposition will see your Christlike hearts.

---

tation that further loss will occur or a desperate longing for "luck" to spare them further destruction.

The Christian can and should look with hope to the future, even if it is hope in the next life. The Christian being interviewed on TV during a crisis should always be able to express what the non-Christian cannot—that there is something better in the future.

Again, the nonbeliever watching the interview at home will look on with skepticism. Your genuineness must "win him over." Are you prepared for any loss in your life? Can you still remain optimistic of the future despite what tragedies may come your way?

I once interviewed Alan Ahlgrim, a Christian minister, about a tragedy in his church. A couple was losing their child to a heart defect. Ahlgrim responded with, "The people involved are spiritually prepared. They did their preparation in advance. When one hits the water it is too late to learn to swim."[2] This couple already knew how to swim; they were prepared in advance spiritually. They suffered the loss emotionally, but could also maintain a trust in God when interviewed by TV cameras.

Learn to swim spiritually before the loss occurs. In crises, interviews on TV look with hope to the future.

Be Factual

In the midst of an event interview where something unexpected has happened, it is easy to understand how someone being interviewed could make disjointed statements. Yet those are the interviews where reporters are seeking facts and figures to give viewers an idea of the impact on what has just happened.

How much damage was done by the explosion? How many people will be affected by what happened? When can regular programs be resumed? What are some ways to measure the impact in dollars, numbers, or statistics? These are some questions you need to have answers to when asked for the impact of the unexpected.

The quoting of facts will also allow you to remain calm under the pressure of the moment, which has been made even more intense by the television reporter asking you questions. The best way to know the answers to these questions if a disaster were to occur is to know thoroughly your organization or church now. Research every area relating to your group, its history, its growth, its current statistics and future plans. Nothing beats preparation, not even a tragedy to your organization and the added pressure of a live television interview that may result from it.

When I was anchoring the evening news program at a TV station in Cincinnati, the Rollman Psychiatric Institute suffered a loss of heat in the dead of winter. The station arranged for a live interview with an administrator of the hospital. When the administrator was questioned about the impact of the heating loss, he was able to give detailed information on how many patients were affected, what steps were taken to insure the health of patients and staff, and when operations would return back to normal. He knew the answers to those questions on a moment's notice because he was well versed with the operation in advance of the mishap. It was then easy to "fill in" any holes in information quickly because he had the basics well in hand.

Learn everything you can about your operation in advance of the unexpected. That will allow you to be factual when the unexpected occurs.

Be Expressive

Evangelist Jimmy Swaggart debated a representative of the People for the American Way on CBS television on Sunday night, February 3, 1985. During the debate, the two were asked to respond to various social questions. Among them was abortion. It was clear to Christian eyes which man represented the biblical position on taking the life of an unborn baby—Jimmy Swaggart.

At one point in the debate the representative from the liberal organization said he too was speaking from biblical terms of "love." To present his ideas on how God will seek judgment on those who take the lives of the unborn, Mr. Swaggart said, "Here, take this Bible, hold it up and tell us how you have supported the killing of millions of babies."

Effective? Yes! That expressive display of how Swaggart personally feels and how hypocritical the other man was in claiming to speak Christian love while taking lives through abortion said more in fifteen seconds that many of us can say in hours. Seek ways to be expressive in what you say for the Lord.

Remember also that there is value in being oppositional over matters of the Word. You *must* speak the Word in fullness and truth. Don't seek confrontation, yet when it arises (as it did in the debate on abortion) you are fully justified in being as direct as Swaggart was.

In all interviews be expressive. When the circumstances demand it, be confrontational. Do not confront individuals in anger or resentment, but face the issues head-on.

Be Controlled

It doesn't matter what your circumstances are—you must remain controlled. Don't take that to mean "unemotional." A genuine display of emotion is important to your effective communication through the medium of television. You must be in control of what you say and how you say it. Display emotion when necessary, but know what emotions you are displaying and how you are being received. Control your emotions when faced with a negative situation such as a serious event that has affected you or your church, such as a fire. You can be emotional over your loss, yet still be controlled.

Your being controlled with your situation will also help you maintain control over the interview process. The best example of control under pressure from my personal experience comes from Senator Jeremiah Denton. He is controlled under fire, yet full of conviction. He knows what he is saying and how he is saying it—and thus controls the interview process.

Once while being interviewed with some other people

concerned about prayer in school, Denton was confronted by a rude reporter. The Senator told the press that he had a statement and that some others had statements and then they would take reporters' questions. The insulting reporter said, with no consideration of the position Jeremiah Denton held, "Wait a minute, Senator, you don't make the rules here. I want to ask a question now [of one of the other speakers]." At this point Senator Denton with great calmness, assurance, and hospitality said, "Well, we'll follow the plan as outlined," and immediately introduced the next speaker.

You cannot afford to let reporters take control of you or of the situation. You must remain detached from the situation and don't respond to what takes place in the interview with a loss of control. That will spell sure defeat.

When in an interview, remain controlled. Here are a few tips on how to keep control during an interview.

- *Command attention* with "humble confidence." You should show the love of Christ when you speak and do so with strength.
- *Set the parameters.* Say what areas you will discuss during private interviews, talk show appearances, press conferences and the like. Set time limits where appropriate and set a limit to the number of questions any one reporter can ask.
- *Be well-groomed.* A carefully groomed appearance will show authority and will be treated with respect.
- *Be cautious of pauses and "uh's."* Any hesitation on your part will indicate you are ill-prepared and will give reporters opportunity to ask another question before you have sufficiently answered the first one.
- *Be concise/Begin again.* Your answers should be concise and to the point. When you do make a mistake or pause excessively, start the answer over again. There is no need to announce that you're going to do this ... just do it.

- *Be clear.* Use understandable language, so the reporter will not have to ask for clarification and throw you off track.
- *Be personable.* Always maintain warmth and friendliness.
- *Be Christlike.* "How would Jesus handle this situation?" should always be the first question you ask yourself.

---

[1]Oswald Chambers, *Approve of God*. London: Oswald Chambers Publishing Association; published by Marshall, Morgan & Scott, 1975, p. 124.

[2]Personal conversation with Alan Ahlgrim in February, 1983.

CHAPTER 7

Other Television Opportunities

Editorials

Editorials are an excellent way for Christians to speak on television and address the concerns of their communities. The Federal Communications Commission has tried to encourage local TV stations to use editorials as a forum for discussing the pros and cons of a given topic. Christians have not taken as much advantage of this forum as possible.

Much of the public debate on many topics in our world today reflects some ignorance of the Word of God. Certainly, much of the controversy over topics like abortion, genetic engineering, pornography, and so forth springs from an ignorance of what God would have us do with the world we were given to oversee.

It would be rare to find a local television station debating the pros and cons of nuclear disarmament. It would not be rare to see a community discuss through the media the controversy of abortion as it relates to the opening of clinics in that city. A good example of that debate was seen when the Archdiocese of Albany, New York sought media attention for its opposition to two abortion clinics in the Albany area. Reverend Michael Farano, the Chancellor of the Archdiocese, spoke against the clinics and said the church was on "solid ground" in its opposition to them. Abortion clinics are in most communities. What are Christians in those communities doing about them?

Speaking in a television editorial is more precise than responding to a reporter's question. You will almost always be using a written script. The script will generally be retyped for a teleprompter. For those who have not used a teleprompter before, it is a device allowing the presenter to look at the lens of the camera and to read his script as it appears on the glass in front of the camera lens.

Keep the following suggestions in mind before recording the editorial at your local television station.

1. Prior to going, confirm with the editorial director of your local station that you would like to use a teleprompter.

2. Find out from the representative how much advance time is needed to retype your script onto the prompter paper. Send a neatly typed copy well in advance of the time that is necessary to retype the script for the prompter.

3. Time the script you send to the station. It should not exceed the allotted time you have been given to address the topic.

4. Address the topic, not the opposition. The editorial time should be used wisely and with love, not as an opportunity to denounce those representing the other side. Let the strength of your message on behalf of your side of the topic persuade the audience, not personal accusations or attacks.

5. Request that you be given sufficient practice time to become familiar with the retyped script (it will appear different once retyped on prompter copy). Check the retyped prompter script for errors, especially those that may change the substance of your message. Use the

practice time to rehearse your delivery and to become familiar with the studio environment and the cues from the cameraman or floor director. I recommend not more than fifteen to twenty minutes prior to the actual taping of the editorial. This should be sufficient time to accomplish what you need to get done, yet brief enough not to infringe upon the hospitality of your local television station.

6. Once the taping begins you are in control. Be satisfied with the copy that will be aired. This may require a few "takes," but it is your message. Firmly request that you be allowed to continue the taping until you are satisfied. Most television stations are accommodating in these matters. A polite request to "do another take" will usually be met with approval. After all, you will be on their station; they too want a professional editorial as the finished "product."

7. Follow up the editorial with a personal, handwritten note to the station representative who worked with you on the taping. This is important. Indicate that you will be willing to address other editorial topics that touch on church issues in the future. If you are an effective representative of the religious community, you will be asked back on other occasions.

Community issues could and should be addressed through the medium of television. Look for the issues of local interest and utilize the opportunities provided by communications law in this country to address them through editorials.

The Church's Use of Video

Few churches have considered producing a videotape "profile" that presents their people, programs, and facilities, even though such a profile is simple and inexpensive to produce and can be used in many ways.

Follow these steps in getting a videotape made of your church.

1. Contact local production houses. Tell them you want to produce a five-minute program about your church. Ask them to give you quotes for production costs including shooting the video tape, production assistance with writing the script, narration costs, editing fees, and any post production you may want. Also make sure the church keeps all raw footage of the church and its activities.

2. Ask them to formally contract for this "production package" and be sure that they have left nothing out of the estimated costs. An estimated cost should be two to three thousand dollars for a five-minute documentary with three copies of the finished product and with all tapes of unedited footage. Don't pay more than this. You may want to contract with the production house that your church will not pay more than a certain sum for the entire production. Remember also that cheapest is not always best.

3. The tape should clearly identify your church. Where possible show a sign with the church's name. Be sure to have people in virtually every shot, since you want to highlight the members of the church. You will want the tape to show love and warmth. If some of the members want to "clown" a bit while making the tape, put that unscripted material in the tape. Don't lose sight of the fact that this is a reflection of your church, not a solemn documentary.

4. Where possible use church members for narration, technical support, and scripting, but insist that an outside professional oversee the production. This will insure a good working relationship with an objective viewpoint of the production's goal and limitations.

5. Once the videotape is produced, look for ways to get local stations to use it. Use portions of the video presentation

- when you have a public service announcement on a local station.
- when bringing people into the church for possible membership.
- when a news story airs that relates to your church.
- when the local station needs to use the tape for their "cover video"

Public Service Announcements—PSA's

Like editorials, PSA's are ways of getting important church information out over the airwaves at no cost to the organization, yet they too are little used. Many local television stations will cooperate with your organization or church if you call well in advance of the date of your event. Find out the procedure of getting a message on the air, when it will air, and what information you need to give the station.

In using PSA's keep in mind the following suggestions.

1. If the announcement is to be read by a station representative along with other announcements, be sure the information you give the station is accurate. The station will air what you send them. They will not know if some of the information is erroneous.

2. Where possible ask the station to air part of the video you have produced about your church while the announcer is reading the information about the upcoming event. The video will add much to your announcement and make it stand out among the other announcements.

3. Churches should look for opportunities to use professional PSA's as ways of promoting their own programs. For example, a nationally produced thirty-second tape on the dangers of lung cancer could be followed with a "tag" that a cancer seminar will be held at your

church on a given date. A tape on drunk driving could be used to announce your church's sponsorship of an ongoing meeting of A.A. or "contact group" to discuss alcoholism. PSA's are also readily available from national organizations.

Be creative in how you use video PSA's and in the ways you use your church facilities to bring people into contact with your church. A creative use of video through television PSA's can dramatically increase the use of your church's physical plant.

Organization

Begin compiling a "media results file" for your church. Always save at least five copies of any article that appears in print, always tape record radio reports, always get VHS or Beta copies of any TV report. Be sure that the copies are of good enough quality to be copied again at some later date if needed.

Designate one person to lead your media/news contact team. This person should be excited about the opportunity to serve in this role. He should not view the job as something that has to be done but no one else wants to do. The success of any media contact team will largely depend upon the enthusiasm the members have for their projects.

CHAPTER 8

Radio and Print Media

Most of the suggestions offered in this guide have pertained to television news. While that medium should not be the only one used by church leaders, it is the one most widely depended upon by most Americans. According to a report by Radio-Television News Directors' Association on future trends in journalism, news consumers can be categorized by reliance on one medium more than another.

At the present time, a majority of all persons (54%) claim to depend on television to obtain news and information. A quarter rely most on a daily newspaper, while 14 percent name the radio and 2 percent, magazines. Use of newspapers and network TV is greatest among those who are most interested in following the news. Those who are less interested more often rely on local TV.[1]

We might conclude, then, that church leaders wanting to reach more people should use television more than other media. However, because of the constraints placed on each medium, that conclusion could result in less public awareness than we could have by using a variety of media.

Church leaders can maximize their effective use of news media by *not* relying exclusively on television. The Christian message and perspective can be presented in many other ways through other media.

Radio News

Radio has some unique characteristics that make its use very attractive ... even more attractive than television for some subjects and at certain times.

Two-thirds of the news directors [of the Radio-Television News Director's Association] when asked what they see as the main advantage of radio news compared with television news, said that radio was more immediate, a faster source of information than television. One in five said that news could be presented more frequently on the radio than on television. Other advantages of radio identified by radio news directors include radio is simpler technically, is more available to the listeners, can do more in-depth coverage, and is 'more interesting.'[2]

Each of the points suggested by most news directors can be viewed as a unique characteristic of radio, which could help church leaders use that medium more effectively.

Radio Is More Immediate
This aspect of radio is perhaps the most important for church leaders to consider. Churches have long been aware of the importance of using radio as a means of carrying worship services and evangelistic messages. This same quality of immediacy can be used when trying to reach users of radio news. There is no better news medium than radio for immediacy because it is easy for radio reporters to set up live reports and because many

more people have access to radios than televisions during the day.

Many radio reporters have the technical capability to "feed" live reports back to their stations from the scene of your local event. Thus, a little coaching of the radio reporter in the importance of any event of which your church is a part could result in that reporter "going live" from your event. That would result in tremendous immediate awareness of what your church is doing at that special time. Remember the number of commercial businesses that have used "live remote broadcasts" to enhance the flow of customers through their stores during sales events. In fact, one of the promotional announcements radio stations used themselves to attract new advertisers is "Radio Works."

More In-depth Coverage

Because there are many more radio stations in a given city than television stations, church leaders have more opportunities to present their messages as part of the regular programming of some of those radio stations.

> All-news radio stations ... are perfect vehicles for opportunities for spokespersons from your organization to appear on locally produced interview shows. [All-news radio has] a considerable amount of air-time to fill and [is] often looking for input from organizations like yours. You should have more than one spokesperson available for this to avoid any possible scheduling conflicts and to offer stations a variety of types.[3]

All-news radio stations and other stations that want to present community issue programs are always "hungry" for content. Because radio can give more time to the church leader, there can be greater discussion of any given topic. The church leader representing his ministry should be prepared when being interviewed on radio to explore topics in more depth than when he is on television. While it is true that he may also have to follow the same guidelines of succinctness outlined for television interviews, he could be granted considerably more time on radio than he would be on television.

Actively seek stations, programs, and reporters in the radio industry who will grant you air time to present your views on topics about which your church is concerned.

Radio Is "More Interesting"

Perhaps this is because more imagination is used when listening to a radio report than to a television news report. Decades ago the use of imagination was a key ingredient in the success of radio serial programs. Many Americans have lost that sense of creative thought when viewing news on television. Yet radio news once again allows the listener to form his own mental pictures of what is happening as the radio report is given. This fact can work as an advantage to church leaders when they are interviewed on radio.

The church leader being interviewed by radio should use visual language when describing scenes, events, and activities. By so doing the church leader will help the listener use his own mental images to picture what has taken place. This can be very important psychologically. When the listener uses his own mental pictures, there could be less resistance to what the church leader is saying. The language chosen for the radio interview should be carefully considered so it will not present a wrong or offensive mental image.

Ways to Enhance Radio Use

TV is a visual medium; effective TV interviews and reports have exciting pictures. With radio interviews, a different sense must be highlighted—hearing.

Your organization should be able to provide radio

stations with sound recordings (preferably audio cassettes or reel-to-reel tapes) of the activities of your group. Radio reporters will then be able to use these sound recordings as "background" for their reports. Such recordings could include: church music, choir performances, rallies, speakers' messages, and other sounds that are pertinent to effective "mental visualization" of what you want the radio listener to perceive while listening to the radio report.

Be creative in your use of sound recordings for radio reports. Here is where you can create an image for your organization and accomplish what we emphasized earlier: giving the reporter what he needs to produce a good report. That factor is an important consideration in radio, just as it is in TV.

Your organization should make these recordings available to radio stations when anything newsworthy occurs at your church. Regularly record worship services, special performances, rallies, and so forth. File these recordings according to topic for ready reference during times when you need "sounds that represent your activities."

A second reason to regularly record activities of your church is to produce a library of speakers' messages. This can be useful when a radio station needs a statement from your church on an issue and a spokesperson is not available. Major ministries do this frequently when time will not allow their minister to be interviewed by reporters. The larger the library of speakers' messages, the more variety you can have when giving these recordings to radio stations.

Radio Station Checklist

____ Exercise similar pre-interview contacting of reporters as described in the Office Interview section, p. 37.

____ Speak in "word pictures" that will help the listener visualize what you are saying.

____ Prepare a "sound library" of recordings of your organization's activities.

____ Prepare a "speakers' library" for opportunities when you can provide excerpts for use on radio.

____ Speak even more succinctly than when on television. With radio, reporters can more easily "splice" two answers together because of the absence of pictures. Exercise more control over what you say by making the answers brief. This will allow you more clarity of a single thought and it will allow reporters the option of "butting" two of your answers together.

Print Media

Print media gives church leaders and publicists special opportunities to present messages that broadcast media do not. The Independent Sector, a umbrella public relations concern in Washington, D.C. for over five hundred private, social, and charity organizations, suggests seven avenues of print promotion and announcements. Each of these has unique features and certain guidelines to follow.

Editorials

Local newspaper editorials are far less used by Christians than they ought to be. Make a regular habit of presenting your church's views before newspaper readers through editorial responses.

> Contrary to general belief, editorials are not always initiated by media management. It is possible to convince a news organization of the validity of doing an editorial on your issue. Often you can be successful in preparing an editorial on your subject and getting a newspaper, or radio or television station, to run it. This should involve a personal visit by you and your

key executive to the top management of the news organization. Be sure to have plenty of background material that provides additional details to support your cause.[4]

Persistent effort is necessary in some cases, but the result will be worth it.

Feature Stories
Creativity is a key in writing feature stories for newspapers and magazines. How can your church or organization make an impact in a number of areas? What is your church's position on politics, economics, social problems, and other issues that serve as categories of feature stories? Here the Independent Sector suggests,

> Because newspapers (and magazines) now have a large variety of departments, you should consider developing a different type of story for each of these sections. You should look into the possibility of preparing or suggesting individual feature stories for the business, metropolitan, entertainment or sports sections on issues regarding your organization.[5]

This idea challenges church or charity publicists to seek ways in which they can better present their message in a number of forums.

Letters to the Editor
Letters to local newspapers can be ways of responding to views from the newspaper or community with which your organization disagrees. These letters should take the form of a serious, well-thought-out response and not an emotional harangue.

The number of letters sent to the editor should be a matter of calculated strategy. On some occasions, the larger the number the more impact. On other occasions, one well-drafted letter can accomplish far more. Public outcry should be measured in direct response to the sensitivity of the issue. For example, deeply emotional issues such as abortion should be dealt with by a single well-thought-out response. An issue such as school prayer would lend itself to mass mailing the editor letters supporting your organization's view. The sensitivity dictates the response.

Op-Ed or By-Line Pieces

More sophisticated news organizations have developed Op-Ed sections for members of the public to respond to suggested topics. This can serve as an excellent opportunity for you or your organization to write a well-produced article presenting a view on a topic. The Independent Sector suggests that preparing such an article in your name will help your community become more aware of your organization's active involvement.

Annual Reports

While annual reports are not as effective at presenting position statements as some other communications avenues are, they can still serve as a library of information about an organization. New members of a community, for example, can profit from a condensed, concise information package about your organization. In your annual reports, you could include position statements about various topics your organization feels strongly about.

> It is extremely important for organizations to be thoroughly understood by their various publics on issues and to convey the hard and meaningful work being done by the group in support of its members. Such an in-depth look at an organization can often be accomplished by an annual report. A publication of this type allows the organization to present areas of interest and concern and to do so without the restraint of time or third-party media interpretation. There is complete

control of such a publication. The message that is printed is the message that the organization wishes to convey, not what someone else decides.[6]

News Releases

News releases have been mentioned earlier in this manuscript. The advice there stands for all forms of media, not just television. It is probably wise to send more news releases to radio stations and print news outlets than television stations because they produce a larger volume of news. Give these sources far more on a regular basis that you would television stations. Print outlets can give your organization a few lines of print or a radio station will give your organization a few seconds of air time when a television station cannot because of their much limited time for news.

Speeches

Your organization should seek to present a speaker at any event where you can get an opportunity. Verbal presentations of your organization to even a small number of people will help build the awareness in your community of the programs of your organization. Take advantage of each speaking opportunity you can.

> After each speech you should take the opportunity to 'merchandise' the appearance by preparing reprints for distribution to news media, your members and interested friends of the organization.[7]

While I do not want to cheapen the gospel by implying that we should "sell" it, I do suggest we use some successful public awareness campaigns to help spread the message.

When a member of your organization speaks, wherever appropriate include a speech summary to news organizations along with a press release to allow news reporters to gain more understanding of the ongoing activities of your group in community affairs. This "reprint" concept is also an effective way for church leaders to build a portfolio of personal references.

Whenever there is an opportunity to share your message with even one person ... do so. You may be sharing it will an "Andrew" who may go and tell some "Peter;" thus your message is spread by a number of faithful believers and not just you. (This is also the most effective way of presenting the gospel itself.)

Ways to Enhance Print Use

The purpose of this handbook is to allow you to gain and maintain more control over media use. The application of specific techniques of media relations with print differ from those of broadcasting, but the goal to be accomplished is the same: a better image of your organization through media use.

Print Media Checklist

Print reporters, as a rule, are more thorough than broadcasting reporters. You need to have more documentation of facts, event dates, times and locations than when you are interviewed by reporters from radio or TV. Print reporters are looking to fill more space than are broadcasting reporters, so naturally they are interested in more detail.

____ Document your ideas and views with facts, figures and quotes from other publications.

____ Supply the print reporter with pictures of what you are talking about. Be careful to use a professional photographer when taking these pictures. Hire a freelance print photographer if necessary. These photos serve the same purpose as videotapes you would give a television news reporter.

____ Be prepared to spend more time with print reporters than with broadcasting reporters. They are more inclined to want to linger at your office or event to get a "feeling of the atmosphere" so they can write about that more effectively. TV reporters rely on their videotape to do this. Radio reporters rely on their sound recordings. Print reporters must rely on their choice of words to convey thoughts and images. This requires more research time. Be patient and understanding of this necessity.

_____ Ask for a copy of the story to preview before publication. Unlike broadcasting, print reporters are more likely to be able to give you opportunity to read their report before publication. Magazines will usually have more time than newspapers to do this. Ask nonetheless for opportunities to read what the print reporter writes so you can catch any factual errors or correct any misrepresentation of fact. Reporters will be reluctant to let you do this, but if you have built a good relationship with the reporter your request to see the story before printing could be answered.

_____ Follow up each article with a note of appreciation or, if necessary, correction of any error that appeared in the article.

_____ Take appropriate response by having your membership express their pleasure or displeasure of the article when such mass response is valuable.

Which Medium to Use?

Each medium—television, radio, newspapers, or magazines—has certain qualities that make it attractive for presenting a message through a news interview format.

- Radio's most significant strength is for providing immediate, quick coverage. Even so, in contrast to the broadcasters' perceptions, more than twice as many persons point to television rather than radio as standing out in this dimension.

- Newspapers do best for providing useful, complete, and in-depth coverage. However, no more than a third of Americans ever cite newspapers as standing out on any single area.

- Magazines are strongest for being concerned with persons like the respondents, for covering controversial issues, and for providing in-depth coverage of the news. However, only a little more than one in ten ever point to magazines as standing out on any dimension.[8]

While you should consider the perception of the public, the structural format of each medium is more important than public awareness in some cases. For example, while most people do not see magazines as a regular source of news, that medium still remains a tremendous forum for reaching a more intellectual segment of the public with time to give serious thought to the message being presented.

Take advantage of a wide range of opportunities to present your message through media. Don't be so selective that you turn down interviews in one medium because you prefer another.

Media Selection Grid

When selecting which medium would be most useful for your message you need to consider factors like these: public dependency, reliability, immediacy, length of coverage, thought time by the viewer/listener/reader, frequency of availability, and perception of genuine concern "for people like me." The following chart is useful in selecting a medium. Keep in mind that using more than one medium is generally best in presenting messages to get a mix of these factors mentioned.

Medium	*Dependency	Reliability	Immediacy	Depth of Coverage	§Thought Time	Appearance Frequency	¶Concern
TV	1	2	3-4	4	4	2	1
RADIO	3	1	3-4	3	3	3	4
NEWSPAPERS	2	3	1-2	2	2	1	2
MAGAZINES	4	4	1-2	1	1	4	3

*(Radio Television News Directors' Association—1983 Survey)
§(Thought time is defined as the length of time to reflect on the message presented)
¶Concern is defined as genuine empathy for the consumer of news of that medium as valued by the RTNDA)

No one medium is best in each category. When you want a message to have immediacy, select radio and/or TV. When you want consumers of a news medium to have more time to reflect on the message, newspapers or magazines would be most appropriate. By using more than one medium, church publicists can maximize the awareness of their messages.

---

[1]*Future Trends in Broadcast Journalism*, Frank N. Magid Associates, Inc., RTNDA Job Study, June 1984. p. 48.
[2]Magid Associates, p. 13.
[3]Independent Sector Press Guide, 1985, Washington, D.C., p. 2.
[4]Independent Sector Press Guide, p. 1.
[5]Independent Sector Press Guide, p. 2.
[6]Independent Sector Press Guide, p. 3.
[7]Independent Sector Press Guide, p. 3.
[8]Magid Associates, p. 50.

CHAPTER 9

Bridging the Spiritual Gap

Although he was not addressing television news reporters, in particular, Oswald Chambers said of the reaction of sinners to the gospel, "Until men get into a right relationship with God, the Gospel is always in bad taste. There is a feeling of silent resentment."[1] In a question and answer session with TV reporters, the reporters more often than not reveal their resentment in the tone of their questioning. This causes many Christians to feel they are being attacked personally. Church leaders need to keep in mind that the world is defensive against the gospel. Given the spiritual profile of most TV news reporters, it is no wonder that they react with skepticism—even ridicule—toward the Christian message.

This should not deter church leaders in presenting the gospel with power and force. The church leader being interviewed should not try to be confrontational, but should not take opposition as a personal affront. In fact, while under fire from skeptical reporters disregarding the church leader's message as nothing more than uninformed ignorance on true liberal thought, the Christian should remain firm in conviction and determination to represent Christ. Paul before his accusers gives a good example of how this should be done (Acts 17:16-34).

The following should be your concerns when speaking directly to people about a problem:

1. *Begin where the audience is.* Get in step with the people with whom you want to communicate. This beginning technique in public speaking is appropriate in dealing with TV audiences, even though it is difficult because of the size and diversity of the audience.

When he spoke before the people on Mars Hill, for example (Acts 17), Paul began by noting that they were a very religious (superstitious) people. They worshiped various gods and were aware that there might be a god that they were neglecting to worship, so they erected a statue to the "unknown god."

The true God was unknown to these people. Only after Paul had gained their attention he told them he was there to proclaim to them what they wanted to know—more about the unknown God. Had Paul immediately condemned the people for their ignorance, their reaction may have been different.

2. *Cover each step.* Reporters are probably unfamiliar with spiritual matters. Take them through each logical step to your conclusions. Remember also that many may not see the "logic" in what you say.

3. *Be gracious.* Do not be curt or abrupt with the press. Every Christian speaker should be attuned to the sensitive communications process in which we participate. If there is a breakdown in communication between you and the reporters, let it not be the fault of our human error or abruptness.

4. *Don't worry about results.* When you have made every attempt to present your message in fullness and in love, you have discharged your responsibility. The results are then in the hands of the Lord.

In every biblical record of God-ordained messengers, reward or condemnation from God did not depend not on the results of the message, but on the messenger's willingness to do what God had instructed. Our reward will be given only when we submit to the call of the

Lord. Be as powerful and as direct as the Lord leads you to be in presenting your message.

The majority of TV reporters will not accept the gospel

Case Study #8

Date: January 5, 1984
Location: Campbellsville, Kentucky
Principle: David Fryear, Superintendent of the local school system
Sketch of Events: Superintendent Fryear successfully circumvented the 1980 decision by the U.S. Supreme Court that ended the posting of the Ten Commandments in schoolrooms. Fryear posted quotations of famous Americans that contained references from the Bible. Fryear is confident that new members of the Supreme Court would reverse the earlier decision.

The lesson from Fryear is his shrewdness and creativity, not only in showing the weakness of the Supreme Court ruling, but in dealing with the news media.

He accomplished the end he wanted, the presentation of biblical thought in a secular environment. His creativity gained the attention of the news media by showing them that counterpoints can be scored within the framework of the law—and while holding one's anger or frustration. Had Fryear angrily accused the Supreme Court justices of error, he might have been discredited. In addition the topic might have shifted from the issue of religious freedom of speech to Fryear's own anger at the Court.

When showing someone's weakness of thought, do so with all good intention. No one likes to be told he is wrong. We all like to think we are right. Granted that these are spiritual matters with which we deal. But again, we must realize that the world does not know what Christians know. If they did, perhaps they too would be believers.

Think out effective ways to present your message before the media. Execute those plans after you have calmed down from any frustration or anger you may feel—regardless of how legitimate it may be for you to feel that way.

or your message. That does not mean that they will not give you a fair presentation in their news reports.

There seems to be a feeling among many church leaders that they must convert the news reporters they come in contact with before their message can be given a fair and honest presentation. The power of the gospel message when applied to social issues is from God. His Word will not return to Him void. While the messenger in the form of the TV reporter may not grasp the eternal truths of the church's position on a social issue, the audience at home will still be affected positively by the Word of God. Paul said in Philippians that even when some men were preaching the gospel for selfish gain, the Word of God was still affecting people as God intended.

Even though the interview process is to present the message of God, as it pertains to some social issue, to a TV audience, keep in mind that you may be in a position to plant a seed with a TV reporter that could germinate and result in his salvation. This is why it is important for Christians not to become angry at reporters even when they are offensive and derisive in their attitudes.

Regardless of the outcome, the Christian should always remain firm to what the Lord wants from him. Our job is to plant the seed, not to count the harvest. Even if the reporters reject the message and the audience thinks we're wrong in our positions on the issues being debated, that should not be our concern. God gives the increase. Our concern should be whether our position is correctly based upon Scripture and whether we have presented it as accurately as we can. God will take care of the rest of the communications process.

The Messenger and the Message

It is altogether understandable that in the heat of the moment during a television interview, a Christian may lose the perspective that the message is what matters, not the messenger. You should avoid this pitfall. Having a quotable quote is a good way to catch the attention of the reporters, but the important thing is the message, not how clever you are.

A good example of what I am talking about is what Clarence Pendleton, the Chairman of the New Civil Rights Commission said about a "Comparable Worth" law. Pendleton said that idea was "the looniest idea since Loony Tunes came on the screen."[2] That is what made the headlines and what was on the air. While the quote got Pendleton's face in the papers and on the air, the quote said so much about his message on that subject. Highlight the message. The coverage of the messenger will take care of itself.

I have also seen capable, knowledgeable, loving church leaders become so disturbed by television news cameras and so intimidated by news reporters that they take on the appearance of the world. Perhaps that is blunt, but when church leaders scream and shout in anger as loudly as their worldly counterparts, I can't help but wonder if the world can see any difference between the Christian and the non-Christian.

Christians should be the most skillful communicators of all. The Lord gives us the power we need to do His will. We seek to forget self—yet self-centeredness is what causes us to be less effective at representing God through television than we want to be. Dr. Batsell B. Baxter, one of my early Christian college teachers, said in his book, *Speaking for the Master*, that when nervousness impedes our speaking it is because we have taken our attention off Jesus and placed it upon ourselves. Are we thinking too often about ourselves rather than about our task? Is our first concern that of how we appear, rather than how the Lord appears through us? We must realize that our performance on television news should be judged on how well we represent Christ, not how we present ourselves.

Too frequently today Christians want to make themselves the "stars" of the moment as if they were bringing about some great accomplishment for the Lord. The single best advice for a Christian being interviewed on television is to keep his sense of humility. The size of the forum does not mean that he is now a media celebrity rather than a servant of God. If the Lord has called you to minister to one person privately or to millions of viewers by television, thank Him for the opportunity to serve just the same. Don't let the lights and the camera fool you into believing that any of us Christians are more than mere vessels for His use.

Final Thoughts

Good public relations do not just happen. Success in dealing with news media requires much thought, prayer, and planning. The suggestions made in this guide are for the purpose of helping give some structure to what is being done in media relations. These are only suggestions. They should be taken as ideas from one who wants to see the church better represented in news reports. Nothing in this guide is meant as criticism. Everything is meant for the glory of God.

If we master the techniques of effective use of television, our attention will not be upon the mechanics. Then the love of Jesus in us will be allowed to come through—even on television.

Persevere through the hard times. No organization can expect one hundred percent good press. Keep in mind the realities outlined earlier of the estrangement of the church from the world and the distance between news reporters as a group and members of the church. Any success with media relations should be celebrated. No defeat should be viewed as final. Never let down. Always seek more press, always try to find one more vehicle to present your group's message, always see the next reporter as someone to help you get your point across.

May God bless you in your efforts to share His message of reconciliation to a lost and dying world.

---

[1]Oswald Chambers, *Approve of God.* London: Oswald Chambers Publishing Association; published by Marshall, Morgan & Scott, 1975, p. 39.

[2]Clarence Pendleton, Chairman of the New Civil Rights Commission, from a press conference, November 16, 1984.

About the Author

Rick Taylor is a Washington Correspondent for the Christian Broadcasting Network, Inc. During his 16 years of experience in radio and television, he has covered local, national, and international stories. His current assignment has taken him to the White House, the Supreme Court and to the United States Congress. His career highlights include:

1985   International stories in Hong Kong, Guatemala, Honduras, and El Salvador.
1984   Covered Congressional Prayer Amendment reports and Equal Access
1983   Managed successful media campaign for Christian mayoral candidate
1983   Vice President of Paragon Advertising, Inc.
1981   Covered Iranian Hostage Parade in New York City
1980   Covered Republican National Convention in Detroit
1979   Went to Israel to cover the result of the peace agreement between Israel and Egypt, and reported on the Israel Peace Accords in Jerusalem
1975   Received the Tennessee Associated Press Award

Prior to his work at CBN, Regional Emmy nominated anchor/reporter Rick Taylor worked as prime news co-anchor at WLWT-TV, Cincinnati, Ohio, and WESH-TV, Orlando, Florida. He began his television career at WNGE-TV, Nashville, Tennessee. During his nine years in television news, Rick's reports have been carried nationally by CBN and by distribution through the network of affiliates of ABC and NBC.

Rick's academic training includes graduate work in Mass Communications at Illinois State University and theology study at Cincinnati Christian Seminary and the Howard University School of Religion.